SHILOH

by
Phyllis Reynolds Naylor

Teacher Guide

Written by
Phyllis A. Green

Note

The Dell Yearling paperback edition of the book was used to prepare this guide. The page references may differ in the hardcover or other paperback editions.

Please note: Please assess the appropriateness of this book for the age level and maturity of your students prior to reading and discussing it with your class.

SBN 1-56137-424-5

To order, contact your local school
supply store, or—

Novel Units, Inc.
P.O. Box 791610
San Antonio, TX 78279

Web site: www.educyberstor.com

Table of Contents

Skills and Strategies

Thinking
    Brainstorming, classifying
    and categorizing, comparing
    and contrasting, evaluating,
    analyzing details,
    synthesizing ideas

Writing
    Description, poetry

Vocabulary
    Synonyms/antonyms,
    metacognition

Comprehension
    Predicting, sequencing,
    cause/effect, inference

Listening/Speaking
    Readers' Theater,
    dramatization of dialogue

Literary Elements
    Similes, point of view,
    colloquialisms, theme,
    turning point

Summary of Shiloh:

Shiloh is an abused beagle when Marty Preston meets him while playing in the fields behind his West Virginia rural home. The dog, initially reticent and fearful, warms up to Marty and follows him home. When Marty discovers that Shiloh's owner is Judd Travers, a rather mean-spirited neighbor whose past treatment of animals is suspect, the major conflict of the novel is in place. Marty secretly constructs a pen for Shiloh when the dog gets loose and seeks out Marty. Keeping the secret and providing food for Shiloh are major obstacles for Marty. When a German shepherd jumps the fence into Shiloh's pen and attacks the dog, the conflict intensifies. Judd demands the return of Shiloh and Marty faces some thorny issues. The plot is resolved when Marty catches Judd killing a doe out-of-season and a deal is struck whereby Marty will get Shiloh in return for his silence about the illegal hunting and twenty hours of work for Judd.

About the Author:

Phyllis Reynolds Naylor (born 1933) lives in Maryland with her husband, Rex V. Naylor, a speech pathologist. She has two sons. She graduated from Joliet Community College and American University.

She published her first book in 1965, *The Galloping Goat and Other Stories*. Her first children's novel, published in 1967, was *What the Gulls Were Singing*.

Fiction by Naylor for Children and Young Adults:

The Galloping Goat and Other Stories, Abingdon, 1965.
Grasshoppers in the Soup: Short Stories for Teen-agers, Fortress, 1965.
Knee Deep in Ice Cream and Other Stories, Fortress, 1967.
What the Gulls Were Singing, Follett, 1967.
(Under name Phyllis Naylor) *Jennifer Jean, the Cross-Eyed Queen*, Lerner, 1967.
To Shake a Shadow, Abingdon, 1967.
(Under name Phyllis Naylor) *The New Schoolmaster*, Silver Burdett, 1967.
(Under name Phyllis Naylor) *A New Year's Surprise*, Silver Burdett, 1967.
When Rivers Meet, Friendship, 1968.
The Dark Side of the Moon (short stories), Fortress, 1969.
Meet Murdock, Follett, 1969.
To Make a Wee Moon, illustrated by Beth Krush and Joe Krush, Follett, 1969.
The Private I and Other Stories, Fortress, 1969.
Making It Happen, Follett, 1970.
Ships in the Night (short stories), Fortress, 1970.
Wrestle the Mountain, Follett, 1971.
No Easy Circle, Follett, 1972.
To Walk the Sky Path, Follett, 1973.

Witch's Sister (first volume of "Witch" trilogy), illustrated by Gail Owens, Atheneum, 1975.

Walking through the Dark, Atheneum, 1976.

Witch Water (second volume of "Witch" trilogy), illustrated by G. Owens, Atheneum, 1977.

The Witch Herself (third volume of "Witch" trilogy), illustrated by G. Owens, Atheneum, 1978.

How Lazy Can You Get?, illustrated by Alan Daniel, Atheneum, 1979.

A Change in the Wind (short stories), Augsburg Press, 1980.

Eddie, Incorporated, illustrated by Blanche Sims, Atheneum, 1980.

Shadows on the Wall (first volume of "York" trilogy), Atheneum, 1980.

All Because I'm Older, illustrated by Leslie Morrill, Atheneum, 1981.

Faces in the Water (second volume of "York" trilogy), Atheneum, 1981.

Footprints at the Window (third volume of "York" trilogy), Atheneum, 1981.

The Boy with the Helium Head, illustrated by Kay Chorao, Atheneum, 1982.

A String of Chances, Atheneum, 1982.

Never Born a Hero (short stories), Augsburg Press, 1982.

The Solomon System, Atheneum, 1983.

The Mad Gasser of Bessledorf Street (first volume in "Bessledorf" series), Atheneum, 1983.

A Triangle Has Four Sides (short stories), Augsburg Press, 1984.

Night Cry, Atheneum, 1984.

Old Sadie and the Christmas Bear, illustrated by Patricia Montgomery Newton, Atheneum, 1984.

The Dark of the Tunnel, Atheneum, 1985.

The Agony of Alice (first volume in "Alice" series), Atheneum, 1985.

The Keeper, Atheneum, 1986.

The Bodies in the Bessledorf Hotel (second volume in "Bessledorf" series), Atheneum, 1986.

The Baby, the Bed, and the Rose, illustrated by Mary Szilagyi, Clarion, 1987.

The Year of the Gopher, Atheneum, 1987.

Beetles, Lightly Toasted, Atheneum, 1987.

One of the Third Grade Thonkers, illustrated by Walter Gaffney Kessell, Atheneum, 1988.

(With mother, Lura Schield Reynolds) *Maudie in the Middle*, illustrated by Judith Gwyn Brown, Atheneum, 1988.

Alice in Rapture, Sort of (second volume in "Alice" series), Atheneum, 1989.

Keeping a Christmas Secret, illustrated by Lena Shiffman, Atheneum, 1989.

Bernie and the Bessledorf Ghost (third volume in "Bessledorf" series), Atheneum, 1990.

Witch's Eye (first volume in second "Witch" trilogy), Delacorte, 1990.

Send No Blessings, Atheneum, 1990.

Reluctantly Alice (third volume in "Alice" series), Atheneum, 1991.

Shiloh, Atheneum, 1991.

King of the Playground, Atheneum, 1991.

Witch Weed (second volume in second "Witch" trilogy), Delacorte, 1991.
Josie's Troubles, Atheneum, in press.
The Witch Returns (third volume in second "Witch" trilogy), Delacorte, in press.
All But Alice, (fourth volume in "Alice" series), Atheneum, in press.

Nonfiction by Naylor for Children and Young Adults:

*How to Find Your Wonderful Someone, How to Keep Him/ Her If You Do, How to Survive If
    You Don't*, Fortress, 1972.
An Amish Family, illustrated by George Armstrong, J. Philip O'Hara, 1974.
Getting Along in Your Family, illustrated by Rick Cooley, Abingdon, 1976.
How I Came to Be a Writer, Atheneum, 1978, revised edition, Aladdin Books, 1987.
Getting Along with Your Friends, illustrated by R. Cooley, Abingdon, 1980.
Getting Along with Your Teachers, Abingdon, 1981.

Initiating Activities:
(Several activities are included from which the teacher may choose for the particular class. The
object is to motivate students and to provide a framework for reading the book.)

1. Look at the dedication at the start of the book. What do you predict about the book?
   Why does an author provide a dedication to a book? Do all books have a dedication?

2. What makes a great dog story? Think about dog stories you've read to gather
   evidence to answer the question. Then make some predictions about *Shiloh*.

3. *Shiloh* was the 1992 Newbery Medal winner. Consider these Newbery winners from
   the past: *Number the Stars, Sarah, Plain and Tall, Dear Mr. Henshaw, Bridge to Terabithia*,
   and *Roll of Thunder, Hear My Cry*. What do you expect from *Shiloh*?

4. Ask students to imagine life as a battered dog. Close your eyes and get the feelings:
   You are afraid to approach people lest you be kicked; you are fearful of not being
   cared for—fed, brushed, loved; you don't have a name; you are unable to run about
   and play; you are tied up all the time; you are ridiculed in front of other dogs by being
   kicked and denied food.

5. Look for hints about the book. Hints prepare our minds for the reading, set up our expectations, and get us ready for reading.

Sources of Hints about Books	Information Provided
Dedication	
Title	
Cover	
Teasers on the book cover or in the book jacket	
Recommendations of friends	
Recommendations of experts—book reviewers/award-winning	

Using Predictions

We all make predictions as we read—little guesses about what will happen next, how the conflict will be resolved, which details given by the author will be important to the plot, which details will help to fill in our sense of a character. Students should be encouraged to predict, to make sensible guesses. As students work on predictions, these discussion questions can be used to guide them: What are some of the ways to predict? What is the process of a sophisticated reader's thinking and predicting? What clues does an author give us to help us in making our predictions? Why are some predictions more likely than others?

A predicting chart is for students to record their predictions. As each subsequent chapter is discussed, you can review and correct previous predictions. This procedure serves to focus on predictions and to review the stories.

Use the facts and ideas the author gives.

Use your own knowledge.

Use new information that may cause you to change your mind.

Predictions:

_____

_____

_____

_____

Prediction Chart

What characters have we met so far?	What is the conflict in the story?	What are your predictions?	Why did you make those predictions?

Using Character Webs

Attribute Webs are simply a visual representation of a character from the novel. They provide a systematic way for the students to organize and recap the information they have about a particular character. Attribute webs may be used after reading the novel to recapitulate information about a particular character or completed gradually as information unfolds, done individually, or finished as a group project.

One type of character attribute web uses these divisions:

• How a character acts and feels. (How does the character feel in this picture? How would you feel if this happened to you? How do you think the character feels?)

• How a character looks. (Close your eyes and picture the character. Describe him to me.)

• Where a character lives. (Where and when does the character live?)

• How others feel about the character. (How does another specific character feel about our character?)

In group discussion about the student attribute webs and specific characters, the teacher can ask for backup proof from the novel. You can also include inferential thinking.

Attribute webs need not be confined to characters. They may also be used to organize information about a concept, object or place.

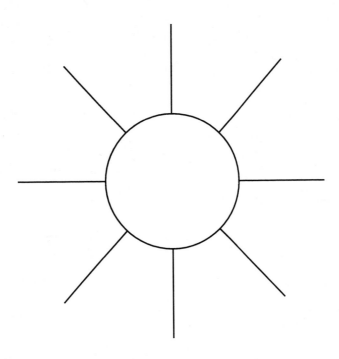

Attribute Web

The attribute web below is designed to help you gather clues the author provides about what a character is like. Fill in the blanks with words and phrases which tell how the character acts and looks, as well as what the character says and what others say about him or her.

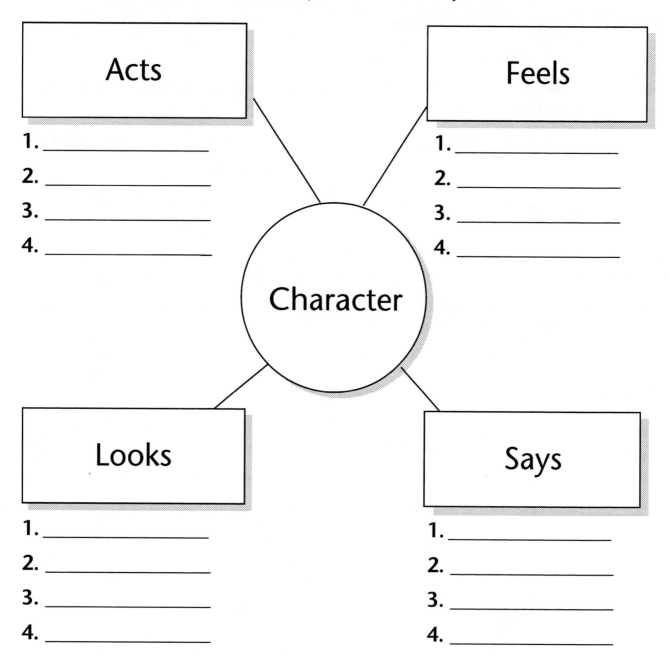

Acts

1. _____
2. _____
3. _____
4. _____

Feels

1. _____
2. _____
3. _____
4. _____

Character

Looks

1. _____
2. _____
3. _____
4. _____

Says

1. _____
2. _____
3. _____
4. _____

Story Map

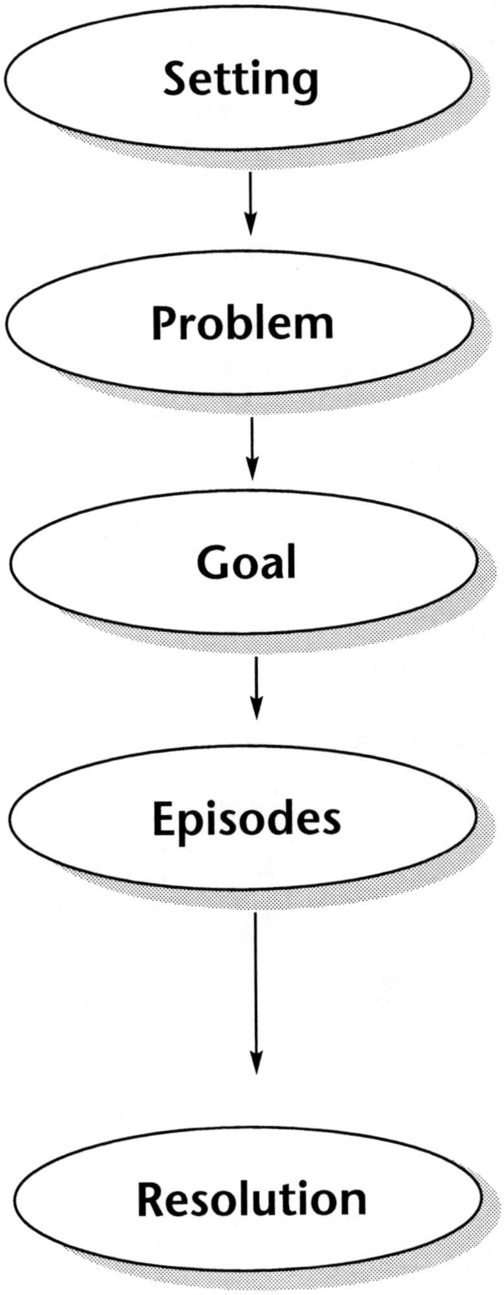

Setting

↓

Problem

↓

Goal

↓

Episodes

↓

Resolution

Characters_____

_____

Time and Place_____

_____

Problem_____

_____

_____

Goal_____

_____

_____

Beginning ——→ Development ——→ Outcome

_____

_____

_____

_____

Resolution_____

_____

_____

_____

Chapter 1 (Pages 11-18)

Plot Summary:
Marty meets Shiloh, an abused dog.

Vocabulary:

groveling 13	whimper 14	cringe 14
whopping 15	ford 15	gristmill 16

Discussion Questions and Activities:

1. Who is telling the story? *(An eleven-year-old from West Virginia; the reader infers that the storyteller is a boy, but Naylor doesn't say that directly in Chapter 1.)*

2. What do you know about the family in Chapter 1? Record on an attribute web. Include references from the book to support your descriptions. (See pages 9-10 of this guide.)

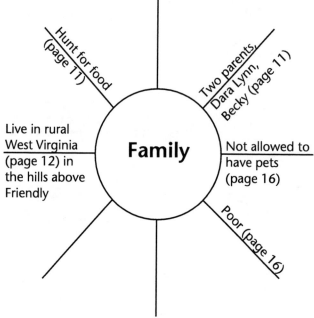

3. Start a simile search in the book. (See page 37 of this guide.)

4. Look carefully at the language in the book. Why are some sentences fragments and some of the grammar incorrect?

5. How does the storyteller name the dog? *(from the place where he met the dog)* Is this a good way to name an animal? Why or why not?

Supplementary Activities:
1. Expand your store of similes by recording interesting similes you've heard or read. Try to use at least one simile in your writing or speaking each day.

2. The author states that the idea for the dog in the story was from a "hungry, trembling, strangely silent" dog that she and her husband met while visiting friends in West Virginia. Where do authors get ideas for their stories? Describe a memorable dog (or pet) you've met.

3. Locate the locale of the story on a map. *(page 12)*

Chapter 2 (Pages 19-27)

Plot Summary:
Marty's father explains that Shiloh must be returned to his owner.

Vocabulary:
loping 20   yelps 27

Discussion Questions and Activities:
1. What do you learn about the storyteller in this story? *(Answers vary, but may include the following: his name—Marty, he's a boy, he's warm and caring towards Shiloh, he's not afraid to speak up to adults, and he understands his father and can predict his reactions.)* Look for evidence in the book for each of your assertions about Marty.

2. What is Marty's attitude toward Judd? *(He dislikes him.)* What are Marty's reasons for his attitude toward Judd? *(He has seen Judd cheat a store owner. He knows Judd chews tobacco and spits near to Marty. Judd stood in front of Marty at the fairgrounds, blocking the view. Judd killed a deer out-of-season.)*

3. Demonstrate the "Friendly, West Virginia" way of getting down to business. *(page 25)*

4. How does Marty feel at the end of Chapter 2? *(sad)* What do you predict for the rest of the story?

Supplementary Activities:
1. What would you do about Shiloh if you were Marty? Answer in a short paragraph.

2. Draw a picture of Shiloh on Marty's lap in the jeep.

3. Compare Judd and Marty's father using a T-chart. (See next page for example.)

Judd	Marty's Father, Ray Preston
Gruff	Matter of fact
Disciplines by whipping	Doesn't want trouble
	Respects the way of the hills
	Respects private property

Chapter 3 (Pages 28-36)

Plot Summary:
Marty continues to think about Shiloh. Marty goes with his dad on the postal route to help deliver the Sears fall catalog.

Vocabulary:

cases 29	froggy 29	sickle 34

Discussion Questions and Activities:

1. What occupies Marty's thoughts in this chapter? *(Shiloh and Judd's mistreatment of him)* Have you ever had something occupy your thoughts in the same way? How did it make you feel? Describe using adjectives or similes.

2. What is Mr. Preston's work? *(postman)* Describe his typical day. *(page 29)*

3. Why does Marty want to earn money? *(to buy Shiloh from Judd Travers)* How successful are his earning efforts? *(He isn't paid to babysit for his sisters. He walks five miles, finding 7 cans and one bottle. Dad finds no other job prospects on his route.)*

4. Compare your leisure activities to those of the Prestons.

You	Prestons
	Catching lightning bugs
	Shooting

5. What are Judd's dog training methods? *(Page 35, He keeps his dogs lean and mean. He doesn't name the dogs or develop any personal relationship. He either calls them or kicks them to go away.)*

6. Why is Marty "so mad I can't see" on page 35? *(Answers vary. He disagrees with Judd's treatment of Shiloh. He is frustrated that he can't change the situation.)*

7. Notice the sentence fragments in the book. Why are they accepted? Is there an understanding as to the complete thought?

Supplementary Activities:
1. Start a story map to record the events of the story. (See page 11 of this guide.)

2. Brainstorm different meanings for the word "case."

3. Start an attribute web to record what you know of Marty's father.

4. Writing: Consider how Marty could solve his dilemma about Shiloh and Judd Travers. "My advice to Marty is..."

Chapter 4 (Pages 37-45)

Plot Summary:
Shiloh runs away from Judd to Marty. Marty decides to keep the dog, building a pen for the dog.

Vocabulary:
warden 38   feeble 39   shadbush 42

Discussion Questions and Activities:
1. What is Marty's dilemma while on the route with his father? *(conflict between respect for adults and their property and supporting what is right and humane, especially as regards the dog Shiloh)*

2. What additional information about the Prestons revealed in this chapter helps to explain their life style? *(The family contributes money for Grandma Preston's care. Money is scarce in the family; there is no money available for feeding and keeping pets.)*

3. "Ma knows me better'n I know myself sometimes..." Explain these words from page 40.

4. How does Judd taking his dogs hunting contribute to the story plot? *(Shiloh runs away to Marty. Marty decides not to return Shiloh to Judd Travers and builds a shelter for Shiloh.)*

Prediction:
How will each of the players in the story react to Marty's keeping Shiloh?

Judd Travers:

Ray Preston:

Mother:

Dara Lynn:

Becky:

Supplementary Activities:
1. Compare yourself to Marty. How are you similar and different? Fill in a Venn diagram.

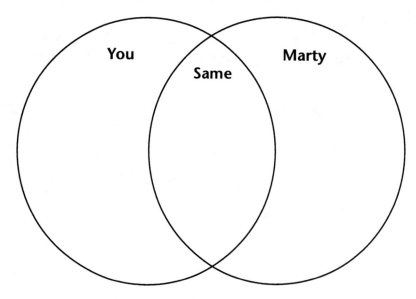

2. How do parents know what their children are thinking? Answer in a short paragraph, using examples from the book and your own experiences.

3. How would Marty finish this sentence? "It's hard to be eleven years old because..."

Chapter 5 (Pages 46-54)

Plot Summary:
Judd asks Marty about his missing dog. Marty skirts the truth in denying seeing Shiloh.

Vocabulary:
   nourish 48

Discussion Questions and Activities:
   1. What words would you use to explain the feelings of Marty and Shiloh on page 47? Defend your word choice.

   2. Why does Marty "stop in his tracks" on page 51? *(He hears a truck motor and is afraid it may be Judd Travers looking for his new beagle.)* Why is "stop in his tracks" an appropriate phrase for this book? *(The setting is rural and hunting and animals figure prominently in the story. The phrase "stop in his tracks" refers to an animal stopping quickly out of fear.)*

   3. How does Marty "dance around the truth" in answering Judd's questions about Shiloh? *(He says he hasn't seen any dogs in the yard or when he went out looking for bottles.)* Did Marty lie?

   4. What is Judd's attitude toward the law? *(He lacks respect for the law and states that in the past the law never controlled his treatment of his dogs and won't in the future.)* What is your personal thinking about Judd and the law?

   5. Will Marty be able to continue to keep Shiloh a secret? In small groups brainstorm possible endings to the story.

Supplementary Activities:
   1. Is Marty justified in hiding the truth about Shiloh from Judd Travers? from his family? Answer in a short paragraph.

   2. Act out this chapter with a simple Readers' Theatre production. Designate the various characters in the chapter, a narrator or two, and a script writer who prepares a short explanation of the situation at the start of the chapter, as well as sentences to explain actions and non-dialogue feelings.

Chapter 6 (Pages 55-65)

Plot Summary:
Lies pile up as Marty provides for Shiloh secretly.

Vocabulary:
> devilment 61

Discussion Questions and Activities:
1. What is the main idea of Chapter 6? Complete this main idea search to support your answer.

    List the major events of the chapter. *(Sunday dinner; put off Ma on inviting David Howard to play; distracted, moody behavior by Marty; prayer; snake story told to Dara Lynn; walk to Friendly; ride from Judd Travers)*

    _____

    _____

    _____

    _____

    List the thoughts of the main character (Marty) in this chapter. *(chocolate bunny incident; lying to family thoughts)*

    _____

    Look for common themes and ideas in your two lists.

    _____

    Are there one or two sentences in the chapter which seem to summarize the main idea? *(Page 60, "Funny how one lie leads to another and before you know it, your whole life can be a lie.")*

    _____

    _____

    Choose a title for Chapter 6.

    _____

2. What does Marty learn about Judd Travers on the ride into town? *(Judd was beaten as a child.)* How does this information help to explain Judd's behavior?

Supplementary Activities:

1. How do you get to a friend's house? How is it similar to Marty's ways? If there are differences, why?

2. Continue adding to the story map and attribute webs. How does this author give you more information and understanding of the characters? Start a Writers' Craft listing or bulletin board. (See page 34 of this guide.)

Chapter 7 (Pages 66-73)

Plot Summary:
Marty spends the day with his friend David Howard.

Vocabulary:

whooping 67   yowls 67

Discussion Questions and Activities:

1. Describe David Howard's home and family. *(page 66)* Why does the author give so much detail about the Howards? *(Answers vary; to emphasize the difference from Marty's family and life style.)*

2. What is Marty's feeling about David's first pet? *(disappointment when he compares the hermit crab to Shiloh)*

3. React to Marty's comment about teachers on page 69 "always looking for ways to make something better than it is." Is the statement true, typical, or fanciful? Share your ideas about teachers, especially from a humorous viewpoint.

4. Look for Marty's thoughts on lying in Chapter 7. *(pages 70 and 73)* On an attribute web, or on another word map, record ideas about lying. Include ideas from the book as well as questions that occur to you.

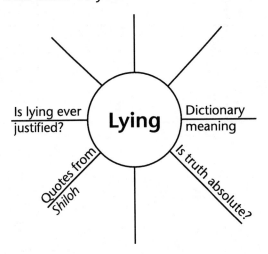

5. Fill in a chart of some problems Marty is finding by keeping Shiloh.

Problem	Marty's Solution	Alternative Idea of Yours
Food		
Storing Food		
Secrecy		
Remembering Lies		
Guilt About Lies		
Mother's Intuition		

Supplementary Activities:
1. Think about David Howard and Marty Preston as best friends. What makes them best friends—similarities, differences, something else? Discuss in a cooperative group and then answer in a short paragraph.

2. What makes a great summer for an eleven-year-old? Think about the question yourself, ask parents or other adults, and then answer in three short sentences.

3. What is a pet? Record your answers on a class word map.

Chapter 8 (Pages 74-80)

Plot Summary:
Ma discovers Shiloh.

Vocabulary:
> gunnysacks 76

Discussion Questions and Activities:
1. What is the "bomb waiting to go off"? *(Page 75, hiding Shiloh; Marty knows that eventually someone will find out.)*

2. How does the author build up to the end of Chapter 8? *(by giving more and more "strange events" which are a result of Marty's keeping Shiloh—food left for Mr. Preston on his route, friends offering headache remedies to Mrs. Preston)*

3. How do the people in Friendly care for those falling on hard times? *(Food appears. Word is passed quietly among friends.)*

4. What is the turning point in Chapter 8? *(Mother discovers Shiloh.)* What is a turning point in a story?

Prediction:
Half the book is still ahead. What will happen?

Supplementary Activities:
1. With a partner, make a list of turning points in various novels. Prepare a game board to share with another pair. List only the turning point and ask the other team to name the novel. For example:

    A sixth grader drowns in a swollen creek. *(Bridge to Terabithia)*

2. How does your community care for those falling on hard times?

Chapter 9 (Pages 81-88)

Plot Summary:
Shiloh is attacked by a big German shepherd.

Vocabulary:

suspicions 82	mistreat 82	yelp 87
snarl 87	bawling 88	

Discussion Questions and Activities:

1. Why does Marty think about how Ma looks when you look up at her when you are down on the ground? *(She looks big and has tree branches in the background. The scene really looks different from the usual vantage and, from Marty's view, the scene is different—Mother is an adult power figure who has discovered Marty in an uncomfortable position.)*

2. On a cube shape (page 23), record the various viewpoints in Chapter 9 and preceding chapters to the Shiloh dog concern. *(Answers vary. Here are some samples.)*

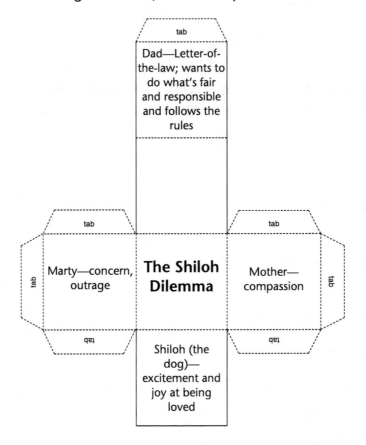

tab

Dad—Letter-of-the-law; wants to do what's fair and responsible and follows the rules

tab

tab

Marty—concern, outrage

The Shiloh Dilemma

Mother—compassion

tab

tab

tab

Shiloh (the dog)—excitement and joy at being loved

Character Cube

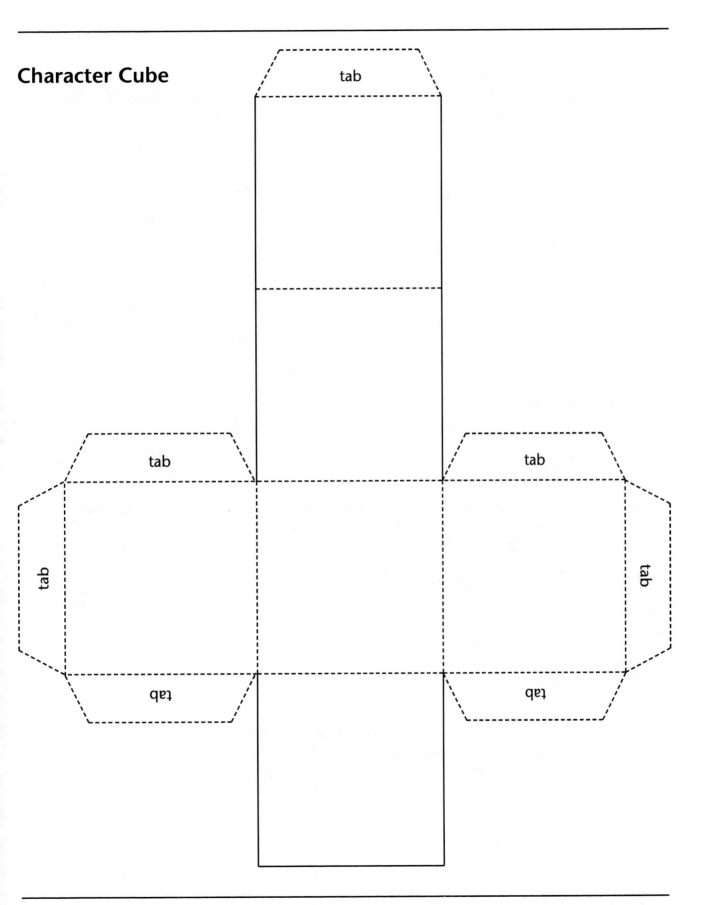

3. This chapter and this book deal with dilemmas in which fairness and kindness are pitted against the legal written rules and the neighborhood customs. Record the balancing attitudes.

Ownership ←――――――――――――――――→ Loving Shiloh

Remaining absolutely honest to Marty's father ←――――――――――→ Support for Marty in his dilemma

Describe some similar dilemmas you've experienced or heard about.

4. What is the accommodation Mother and Marty come to in the matter of Shiloh in Chapter 9? *(Mother will wait one night to tell Marty's father about Marty keeping Shiloh and Marty promises not to run away.)* What are the implications of accommodations? Have you ever experienced or heard about an accommodation?

5. Why does Shiloh yelp in the night in Chapter 9? *(He is being attacked by another dog.)*

Supplementary Activities:
1. "There's two sides to every question." Discuss in regard to Chapter 9.

2. "Ma has a special understanding of Marty." Cite examples from the book to support the statement.

3. Dramatize the dialogue between Ma and Marty in Chapter 9. Use cards for audience involvement to express the feelings in the chapter. (e.g., surprise, shock, happiness, relief) The audience would dramatically but silently emphasize the feelings.

Chapter 10 (Pages 89-95)

Plot Summary:
Dad and Marty take Shiloh to Doc Murphy to be patched up.

Vocabulary:

gunnysacks 89	wince 89	stethoscope 91

Discussion Questions and Activities:
1. Who else is awakened by Shiloh's yelping and howling in the night? How do they react? *(Dad goes to investigate and finds Marty holding Shiloh's bloodied body. Mother gets up and watches from inside the house. Dara Lynn is curious.)*

2. Where does Dad take Shiloh? *(page 91, to Doc Murphy who stitches up the dog even though he asserts, "I'm no vet")*

3. What does the sentence at the top of page 94 mean: "I know then what Ma meant"? *(Looking back to page 83 and what Ma said about trust, Marty understands that a single lie puts into question the liar's trustworthiness. If someone can lie once, what's to stop him from lying again.)*

4. What does Dad seek to teach Marty when he says on page 94, "Open your eyes"? *(There are many injustices and many injustices can't easily or quickly be changed.)*

5. What is the "first time" Marty suggests on page 95? *(the first time for any change or move toward fairness)* Make a list of "first times" you've experienced or heard about. Include personal examples as well as historic and national examples.

6. Why does Dad say that Shiloh may stay with the Prestons until he gets well? *(Answers vary.)*

Prediction:
What will happen to Shiloh? Give support for your ideas. (Hint: How much of the book is left?)

Supplementary Activities:
1. Add to the attribute web for Ray Preston, considering various titles he holds (father, son, postman, neighbor), what his values are, how he takes action.

2. Choose one word to describe Dad's nature. Give examples and reasons for your choice of a word.

Chapter 11 (Pages 96-104)

Plot Summary:
Marty tells David Howard about Shiloh. Doc Murphy returns Shiloh to the Prestons.

Vocabulary:

warble 102	antibiotics 103

Discussion Questions and Activities:
1. What is the style of the author in *Shiloh*? *(informal, storytelling, personal, first-person narrative)* Why is it an effective style for this book? *(fits the plot, location, Marty's age)* Share with your classmates other favorite informal stories.

2. Why does the author on page 97 emphasize the wormy peaches? *(to add details and make the story seem real, to remind the reader of the rural setting and the economic status of the characters)*

3. Marty experiences a variety of emotions in Chapter 11. List the emotions in conjunction with the events described.

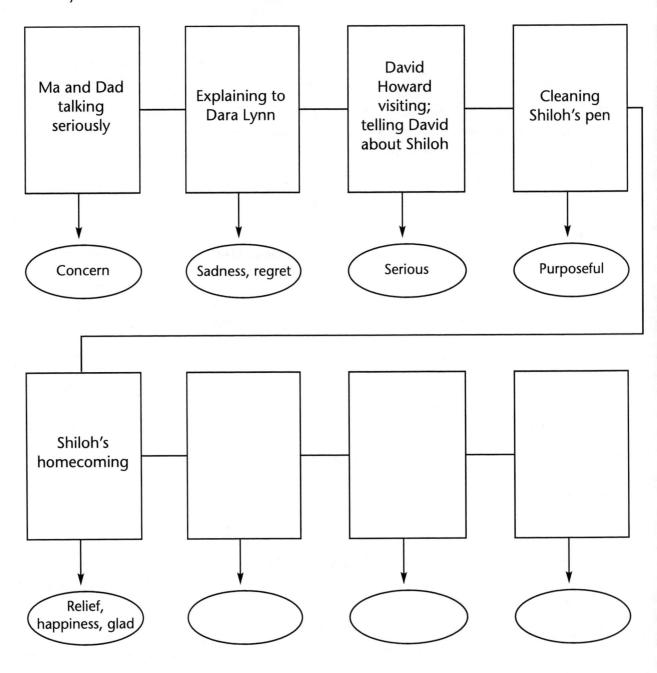

Supplementary Activities:

1. Shiloh gives all the Prestons lots of love. Write a short paragraph to support (or deny) this statement. Use examples from the book.

2. Fill in a graphic organizer about pets.

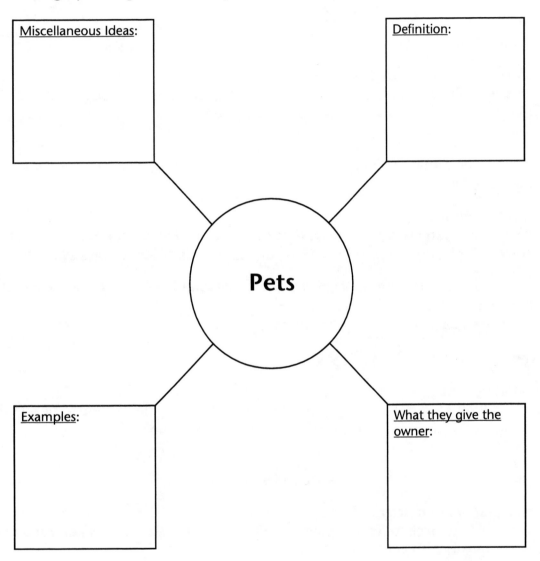

Chapter 12 (Pages 105-112)

Plot Summary:
Shiloh continues to recuperate. Judd arrives at the Prestons' demanding the return of Shiloh on Sunday.

Vocabulary:

      shrieks 106   slurp 106   decency 110

Discussion Questions and Activities:
1. "It's sort of like Shiloh's there and he's not." Explain Marty's thought. *(Page 106, Each family member, in his own way, shows how he likes Shiloh. But Ma and Dad don't mention Shiloh by name.)*

2. What is the climax in Chapter 12? *(Judd Travers drives up, having heard about Shiloh from Doc Murphy.)*

Supplementary Activities:
1. Brainstorm with classmates possible solutions to the Prestons' problem with Judd Travers. Evaluate your solutions. (See page 29 of this guide for one evaluation system.)

2. Collect some of the informal colloquial phrases found in the book. For each phrase, list how you would say the same thing.
      Page 112   "patching him up"

Chapter 13 (Pages 113-119)

Plot Summary:
Marty goes to Judd Travers, planning to plead again for Shiloh. Inadvertently, he sees Judd kill a doe out-of-season.

Vocabulary:

      allergic 115   rehearsed 116

Discussion Questions and Activities:
1. Why is Marty back to not sleeping again? *(He is worried, concerned, and sad about returning Shiloh to Judd Travers.)*

2. What is Marty's problem-solving process in this chapter? *(brainstorming personally and then evaluation for feasibility after collecting any needed additional information)* What questions does Marty mentally ask himself when he considers possible solutions? *(Can I do it? Would the solution give me the result I want? Would the solution get my dad in trouble? How will others—Judd—react?)*

Evaluating Solutions to a Problem

State the problem in a short sentence or two.

Problem	Criterion #1 for evaluation: Does it break any laws?	Criterion #2 for evaluation: Is it quick enough?	Criterion #3 for evaluation: Does it make you feel good?
Solution #1			
Solution #2			
Solution #3			
Solution #4			
Solution #5			

In the boxes, answer the evaluation questions for each solution idea.

3. How does Judd's attitude toward the game and hunting laws affect the story? *(Marty sees Judd shoot a doe out-of-season.)*

Prediction:
What happens next?

Supplementary Activities:
1. Compare Marty to other eleven-year-olds you know.

Other Eleven-Year-Olds	Marty

2. How is animal cruelty handled in your locality? Investigate and report to your classmates. Write to an animal rights group for information.

Chapter 14 (Pages 120-128)

Plot Summary:
Marty confronts Judd and makes a deal to get Shiloh.

Vocabulary:

camouflage 120	weirdest 120	intention 120
warden 120	slogs 120	regulation 122
allowance 122		

Discussion Questions and Activities:
1. How does his assertive, confident nature serve Marty well in Chapter 14? *(He recognizes Judd Travers's illegal deed and tells Judd clearly. Marty then suggests a deal with Judd—Marty's silence for Shiloh.)*

2. How do you feel about Marty's deal with Judd Travers? *(Answers vary, but should include positive and negative aspects—Marty gets Shiloh, Shiloh won't be abused, Marty ignores a crime.)* Do the ends justify the means? Interview parents and others to gain more understanding of the issues posed in the question.

3. Why does Marty ask for his deal with Judd to be written? *(Marty doesn't trust Judd.)*

Supplementary Activities:
1. What makes you happy? What makes the characters in the book happy? Record your answers on a web or other drawing of your choice.

2. Investigate hunting laws in your state and community. Perhaps you can interview a hunter.

3. Discuss with a small group of classmates situations when the question of the ends justifying the means come up.

Chapter 15 (Pages 129-144)

Plot Summary:
Marty fulfills his bargain with Judd and Shiloh stays with the Prestons.

Vocabulary:
omission 130	jubilation 132	squaller 135
whetstone 140		

Discussion Questions and Activities:
1. How does his family react to Marty's news that Judd will sell Shiloh to him? *(happily and with disbelief, surprised that Judd has changed his mind about selling)* Act out the family reacting scene.

2. Make a list of the chores Marty does during his twenty hours working for Judd. *(moves deer to Judd's shed, restacks Judd's woodpile, hoeing, scrubbing down the sides of his trailer and porch, shining up the windows, raking the yard, picking beans, splitting wood, weeding, digging a ditch)* Did Marty make a good deal? Was the deal fair?

3. How does Judd treat Marty while Marty works off his twenty hours? *(badly, nastily, arrogantly)* How does Judd use psychological warfare? *(Answers vary.)*

4. How do Judd and Marty learn to get along? *(Answers vary. Marty doesn't let Judd's nasty manner and attitude push him into reacting in like fashion. Marty learns about Judd's family and feels a little sorry for him. Judd respects Marty's spunk.)*

Culminating Activities

1. Choose a vehicle to summarize the action (plot) in the story. You may use a story map, a game board with each significant action occupying a square, a story pyramid (see page 33), or a paragraph explaining the organization of the story.

2. What makes a character memorable? Map your ideas using webs or other graphic organizers. These questions may help spur your thinking: What book characters do you remember? What do you remember about them? Do you have a vivid picture in your mind of them? Were your memorable characters similar to someone you know?

3. Why was *Shiloh* the 1992 Newbery Medal winner?

4. Choose your favorite chapter to dramatize.

5. What is the moral of the story? Defend your answer.

6. What new facts did you learn from the story?

7. Use the spinner below to choose a writing activity.

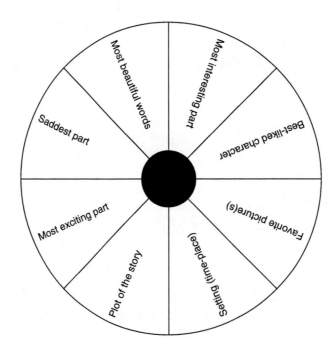

8. Design a poster for *Shiloh*. What will you emphasize? How will you utilize color, line, shape, space, and texture?

Story Pyramid

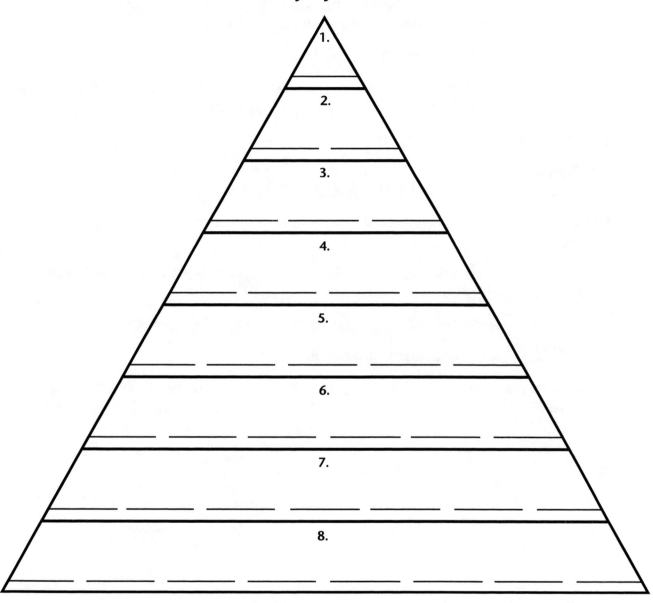

1. One word naming the main character.
2. Two words describing the main character.
3. Three words describing the setting.
4. Four words describing the problem.
5. Five words that represent the first main event.
6. Six words that represent the second main event.
7. Seven words for the third main event.
8. Eight words for the resolution of the story.

9. How will Marty Preston develop as he grows older? Choose a way to share your ideas—an oral report, a written summary, a letter written by an older Marty, a journal written by Marty, or a listing in *Who's Who* for Marty.

10. Write a Bio-poem for Marty. (See page 35 of this guide.)

11. Design a set of community photos of the characters in the book. Feel free to group characters together in whatever way you find appropriate.

12. Create a comic strip of the book.

Bulletin Board Ideas:
(Many of these ideas are included in the Supplementary Activities following each chapter.)

1. Simile Search: List on sentence strips interesting similes from the book or other sources.

2. Writers' Craft: Use a giant pen or quill on which students list ways an author reveals characters and the story to the reader.

3. Story Map: Laminated craft paper allows recording of the elements of the story map.

4. On a huge outline of a beagle, list details about Shiloh.

5. In the center of a web, put a picture of Shiloh. On the stems list what the dog does (verb forms). Around each verb, students finish the verb phrase. (See page 36 of this guide.)

Bio-poem

Directions: Write a Bio-poem for Marty.

—A pattern poem

—Line 1:   First name only
—Line 2:   Four traits that describe that person
—Line 3:   Sibling of ... (or son/daughter of ...)
—Line 4:   Lover of ... (three people or ideas)
—Line 5:   Who feels ... (three items)
—Line 6:   Who fears ... (three items)
—Line 7:   Who would like to see ... (three items)
—Line 8:   Resident of ... (city, state, street, etc.)
—Line 9:   Last name only

—May extend to 11 lines. Between lines 6 and 7 add:

—   Who needs ... (three items)
—   Who gives ... (three items)

1. _____

2. _____

3. _____

4. _____

5. _____

6. _____

7. _____

8. _____

9. _____

10. _____

11. _____

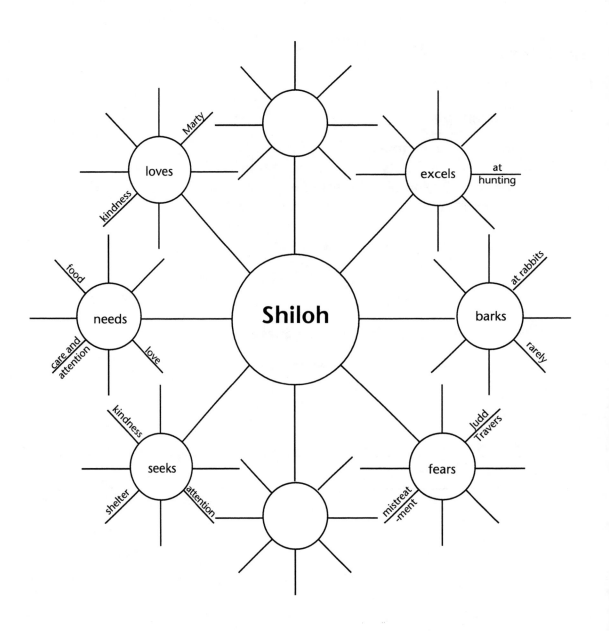

Selected Similes from the Book

Citation	Simile	Compared to
Page 15	"like pressing a magic button"	calling Shiloh
Page 16	"going like a propeller"	Shiloh's tail
Page 21	"like water in a paper bag"	how his dream leaks out
Page 26	"like a window blind in a breeze"	the way Shiloh is shaking
Page 44	"as a cricket"	Marty's tenseness
Page 46	"like a windshield wiper, fast speed"	Shiloh's tail when Marty met him in the morning
Page 55	"like when I stay overnight with David Howard down in Friendly"	lights at night
Page 74	"smooth as buttermilk"	next days
Page 75	"like a bomb waiting to go off"	having Shiloh be a secret
Page 88	"like he's trying to get his tongue out to lick my hand"	Shiloh's actions when he's injured by the German shepherd
Page 109	"like icicles inside me"	Marty's bones
Page 109	"as mean and nasty as I ever seen him look"	Judd Travers in the past

Vocabulary Activities

1. Using the board game on page 39 and the vocabulary words written on 3 x 5 cards, play a game with a partner. Players move around the board according to the throw of a die. To secure his/her piece in the spot, player must provide the required use of a vocabulary word, chosen from the top of the pack of vocabulary cards.

2. Play vocabulary fish. On 3 x 5 cards, prepare a pack of cards. For each vocabulary word, prepare three cards—a definition, a synonym, and use of the word in a sentence. Shuffle the pack of cards, dealing seven cards to each player. Students try to match up triples for vocabulary words which they can put down in front of them. Players ask another player for a specific card, taking an additional card into their hands if they're told to "go fish." The first player to match up all the cards in his hand wins the game.

3. Assign numbers to the 3 x 5 vocabulary cards. Deal out 5 cards to each player who tries to add up cards as close to twenty as possible. To validate cards, and winning, the winner must provide definitions, synonyms, antonyms, or use in a sentence as required by the opponent for each card in the winning hand.

4. Make up a humorous vocabulary quiz for classmates using vocabulary challenge words. For example:

   Would a *muzzle* be a tasty dinner?

5. Use vocabulary steps to guess the vocabulary words. Play with a partner.

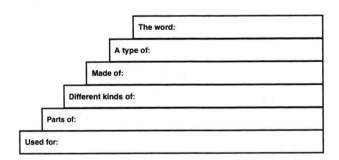

6. Divide class into pairs or groups to figure out ways for classmates to remember assigned words or groups of words. Mnemonic devices, pantomimes, or other tricks are encouraged. Teach your words to classmates.

Vocabulary Board

Finish

Give your word a color; explain.	Put the word into an alliterative phrase.	Give a synonym.
Free space.	Go back 3 spaces.	
Use in a sentence with therefore in it.		Define.
Give an example of the word.	Find a word starting with the last letter.	Give an antonym.
Use as the third word in a sentence.		Use in a sentence.
	Leap ahead 2 spaces.	Give a synonym.

If your word is a noun, go to Finish.

Attach an emotion to the word; explain.

If your word is a verb, cheer and go ahead 5 spaces.

Go back 2 spaces.

Free space.

You're in the dog house; go back 10 spaces.

Use the word in a simile.

Dramatize the word.

Tell the part of speech.

Start

Assessment for *Shiloh*

Assessment is an on going process, more than a quiz at the end of the book. Points may be added to show the level of achievement. When an item is completed, the teacher and the student check it.

Name _____ Date _____

Student   **Teacher**

_____   _____   1. Make your own type of story map for the novel. (See page 11 of this guide.)

_____   _____   2. Complete a simile search for the book.

_____   _____   3. Make an attribute web for Marty's father. (See pages 9-10 of this guide.)

_____   _____   4. Participate in a Readers' Theater production.

_____   _____   5. Compare Marty to other eleven-year-olds you know. Use a T-chart.

_____   _____   6. Divide a sheet of paper into four sections. What are the four most important parts of this story? Draw an illustration for each of these important parts.

_____   _____   7. Complete at least four vocabulary activities.

_____   _____   8. Write the best title for each chapter.

_____   _____   9. Make a mobile of important characters and objects in the story.

_____   _____   10. Write a ten question quiz for a classmate. Make an answer sheet.